[sic]

[sic]

Melissa James Gibson

Garden City, New York

CAUTION: The Stock and Amateur performance rights in the English language throughout the United States, its territories and possessions, and Canada are controlled exclusively by Dramatists Play Service, Inc., 440 Park Avenue South, New York, New York 10016. No professional or nonprofessional performances of the play (excluding first-class professional performances) may be given without obtaining in advance the written permission of Dramatists Play Service, Inc., and paying the requisite fee. For inquiries concerning all other rights, contact the author's agent: Mark Christian Subias, William Morris Agency, Inc., 1325 Avenue of the Americas, New York, New York 10019.

Frank's Very Important Cassette Tape: Grateful acknowledgment is made to The Missouri Auction School for permission to reprint excerpts from "The Missouri Auction School Training Manual." Please apply to Dramatists Play Service for permissson to use the tape in performace.

ISBN: 0-7394-2707-5

Acknowledgments

The playwright would like to thank Daniel Aukin, Linsay Firman, Alexandra Conley, Matthew Frey, Todd London, Mark Christian Subias, and, especially, Melissa Kievman and Elizabeth Giamatti, both of whose insight was essential to the development of this play. Also, thanks to all the actors who have inhabited the play's characters in its various incarnations, and, indeed, informed their evolution.

Playwright's Note

[*sic*] takes place primarily in the doorways and shared hallway of three neighboring apartments; periodically within the apartments; and ultimately on the building's rooftop. The Airshaft Couple was originally imagined as a pair of voices that, in every sense, speak to the main characters from an offstage source, presumably another part of the building. In the production at Soho Rep, however, the Airshaft Couple was brought onstage, occupying an apartment on the floor below those of the main characters. The ceiling of the Airshaft Couple's apartment was very low, so that from all vantage points the audience's view of the actors was obstructed in a variety of ways at all times. In future productions, whether the Airshaft Couple is partially visible or remains a pair of offstage voices, it is vital that the concept of an obstructed view be explored in some tangible sense within the production as a whole. Instead of having the actors in full and presentational sight at every moment, I imagine a scenario in which the visual story is as occasionally fragmentary as the verbal one; wherein, for instance, during selected parts of scenes we watch the action unfold through a half-closed door or a partially open window shade. In this way, the visual perspective of the audience is at times as limited as the outlook of the main characters, whose self-absorption makes them prone to misinterpretation and paranoia at every turn.

Which brings me to the title. [*sic*], of course, is a Latin term that appears in writing, as a signal to the reader that an apparent mistake is in fact an accurate citation. This notion of distancing oneself from responsibility informs the three main characters of the play, who exist at arm's length from their own situations, as if their real lives were yet to be inhabited. (A recipe for dissatisfaction, but there you go.) The main characters are all in their thirties, well past the point when being a wunderkind is a viable option—a fact whose repercussions are very present.

Which brings me to the line breaks, internal capitalizations, and lack of punctuation in general. These are intended as guidelines to the characters' thought processes, in terms of emphasis and pattern; they should be honored, but should not enslave the actors. The cadence should fluctuate according to circumstance and should avoid falling into repetition. The rhythm of the piece as a whole should reflect the momentum of active thought. By extension, during the play's many transitions, solutions other than blackouts should be at all costs sought. Moments should not so much cut in and out as deftly replace one another.

WHO

THEO—in his thirties
BABETTE—his neighbor, in her thirties
FRANK—their neighbor, in his thirties
THE AIRSHAFT COUPLE—somewhere nearby, in their thirties, in dispute
THE VOICE OF MRS. JORGENSON
THE VOICE OF THE DELIVERY PERSON
THE VOICE OF DR. GREENSPAN

WHERE & WHEN

New York City, in a prewar apartment building, now-ish

HOW

The play's language: please see the Playwright's Note on page vii. Also, please note, in terms of the pronunciation of Mrs. Jorgenson's name: Frank pronounces it "Geor-genson"; Babette pronounces it "Your-genson"; and Theo pronounces it "Your-GEN-son," stressing the middle syllable.

Production History

[sic] was commissioned by Steppenwolf Theatre Company as part of its New Plays Lab during the 1997-98 season. It was work-shopped at Soho Rep's Summer Camp in 1999, directed by Melissa Kievman, and was produced by Chicago's Roadworks Productions in June 2000, also under the direction of Melissa Kievman. [sic] premiered in New York City in November 2001 at Soho Rep (Daniel Aukin, Artistic Director, Alexandra Conley, Executive Director, Linsay Firman, Associate Director). It was directed by Daniel Aukin; set design was by Louisa Thompson; lighting design was by Matthew Frey; costume design was by Kim Gill; and sound design was by Robert Murphy. The stage manager was Mandy Sayle, and the assistant director was Eliza Hittman. The cast included Dominic Fumusa, Christina Kirk, Jennifer Morris, James Urbaniak, and Trevor A. Williams.

PART I

From the virtual darkness we hear the sound of a very old woman singing in the shower. She has a throaty voice and sings with gusto:

MRS. JORGENSON'S VOICE:
> Oh I once loved Dick
> but Dick he loved Tom
> Butterflies were worms
> I don't love Dick no more

(We hear the sound of a synthesizer played very slowly; the first couple of bars of a song is played over and over with increasing speed and then with decreasing speed. It sounds like music from an amusement park ride. A phone rings a couple of times. We hear the sound of someone fumbling to pick it up.)

THEO: Are you awake

BABETTE: I was dreaming

THEO: But look outside

(As we see the shadow of a WOMAN *approaching a window blind we hear:)*

FRANK: And when the winter will withdraw the weather won't
         be wild
         And when the winter will withdraw the weather won't
         be wild

And when the winter will withdraw the weather won't
be wild

*(We see portions of a prewar apartment building, primarily four
apartment doors that occupy the same floor, a hallway, a flight of the
building's stairs and part of the building's rooftop.* BABETTE *stands
outside* THEO's *apartment door and knocks.* THEO *answers the
door. They stare at each other for a period of time.)*

THEO: Ten

BABETTE: Twenty

THEO: Ten

BABETTE: Eighteen

THEO: Ten

BABETTE: Twelve

THEO: Ten

BABETTE: Fifteen

THEO: Ten

BABETTE: Fourteen

THEO: Ten

BABETTE: Twenty

THEO: Ten

BABETTE: Eighteen

THEO: Ten

BABETTE: Twelve

THEO: Ten

BABETTE: Fifteen

THEO: Ten

BABETTE: Fourteen

THEO: Five

BABETTE: *(did she hear correctly)*
         Fine

THEO: *(no)*
         Fivvveh

BABETTE: *(without pause)*
         Ten Great Theo Ten Okay Theo Ten Okay Great

         (THEO *opens his wallet, pulls out a ten-dollar*
             bill, and hands it to BABETTE.)

BABETTE: I'll be able to get
         this ten back to you
         well Not This Ten
         obviously Theo obviously but
         A Ten Plus Interest
         sometime uh

THEO: No interest necessary

BABETTE: No it's
         Something I'm Doing
         to clear my Slates
         Debt and Conscience

Thanks Theo
Theo thanks

(BABETTE *retreats from* THEO's *door and enters her
apartment just as* FRANK *emerges from his apartment
and knocks on* THEO's *door.* THEO *answers it.*)

FRANK: I was wondering if I could borrow your
           Cassette Tape Player

THEO: IIII don't have one

FRANK: I wonder who has a
           Cassette Tape Player

THEO: III don't know

FRANK: Does Babette have a
           Cassette Tape Player

THEO: II don't know

FRANK: (*as he walks away*)
           I don't know
           I don't know I don't
           Know how I'm going to listen
           to My Very Important
           Cassette Tape

(THEO *closes his door as* FRANK *knocks on* BABETTE's
door. She answers it.)

BABETTE: Hi Frank

FRANK: Could I borrow hi Babette your
           Cassette Tape Player

BABETTE: I don't have one

FRANK: But what has become of all of the
           Cassette Tape Players

*(FRANK retreats from BABETTE's door. BABETTE closes her door
and then suddenly reopens it as she calls down the hall.)*

BABETTE: Why not ask Mrs. Jorgenson

*(There is the sound of the same short piece of synthesizer
music. PAUSE. And again. Perhaps BABETTE is visible in
silhouette behind her blind. She is searching through the
pockets of clothes that are lying around her apartment.)*

FRANK: *(from his apartment)*
           Sally sought some seeds to sow but sadly soon it snowed
           Sally sought some seeds to sow but sadly soon it snowed
           Sally sought some seeds to sow but sadly soon it snowed

(BABETTE knocks on THEO's door. THEO answers it.)

BABETTE: I'm going to the store downstairs Do you need any-
         thing from The Store Downstairs

THEO: No Uh Yes I need candy bars Could you pick me up
           some Candy Bars

BABETTE: How many candy bars

THEO: Six or seven Candy Bars

BABETTE: Six
         Or Seven candy bars

THEO: Seven Candy Bars

BABETTE: Do you have Uh money

THEO: I just lent you ten dollars

BABETTE: I'm not in a position
           Uh
           Theo think about it
           to antilend
           Just Now

THEO: Antilend

BABETTE: I mean I'd have to be a fool

(THEO *hands* BABETTE *a couple of dollars and starts to close his
door but then stops as he watches* BABETTE *knock on* FRANK's
door. FRANK *opens his door just barely.*)

BABETTE: Do you need anything from the store Frank

FRANK: I need a Cassette Babette Tape Player

BABETTE: The store downstairs Frank

FRANK: Something with Babette which to
           Gargle

BABETTE: Mouthwash Frank

FRANK: For my Babette
           Throat

BABETTE: I'll need the money up front Frank

(FRANK *hands* BABETTE *some money.*)

FRANK: But Babette
           nothing too Harsh

BABETTE: Your throat didn't sound sore last night

FRANK: My throat's not sore

THEO: Last night

BABETTE & FRANK:
           (didn't realize he was there)
           Hi Theo what's uh shaking

THEO: Not much By the way did I hear your doors shutting
           at almost the same instant last night

BABETTE & FRANK:
           Last night

THEO: I think I did

BABETTE & FRANK:
           Last night

THEO: The one that's two nights before tomorrow
           night I think I did

BABETTE/FRANK:
           (each says one)
           You did/Did you

THEO: I'm pretty sure I did and then I happened actually to
           be over by the window and I think I saw you guys cross
           the street together

BABETTE/FRANK:
           (each says the other one)
           Did you/You did

THEO: Yeah and then if I'm not mistaken I saw Frank look up
           at my window and Babette covering the side of her
           face as you both rushed out of view

BABETTE & FRANK:
Oh Theo please we were Here we were Here

BABETTE: *(continues without a break)*
I fell asleep in the middle of a poorly edited epic

FRANK: And I stopped off at Mrs. Jorgenson's

THEO: Funny you should mention Mrs. Jorgenson because I
ran into Mrs. Jorgenson and Mrs. Jorgenson said that
you said that you and Babette were going out for dinner Mrs. Jorgenson also said that you said that you
might try to see a movie Mrs. Jorgenson also said that
you said not to mention any of that to me if Mrs.
Jorgenson happened to see me Mrs. Jorgenson did
happen to see me but Mrs. Jorgenson didn't happen to
remember your request not to mention anything to
me until the details of your evening's plans had fallen
unfortunately from Mrs. Jorgenson's mouth

(PAUSE, *then:)*

BABETTE & FRANK:
It's true we did Socialize without you last night but
only because we were meeting to plan an impromptu
surprise party for you having nothing to do with your
birthday and having everything to do with your being
You Theo You

BABETTE: *(continuing on without a break, irrationally annoyed)*
Now if you'll excuse me I need to pick up some things at
The Store Downstairs

(BABETTE *storms off down the hall.* SLIGHT PAUSE.)

THEO: When's the surprise party

FRANK: *(irrationally annoyed, too)*
            I don't know Theo We didn't get that far but frankly I
            suspect the party's off

*(We hear the sound of the same few bars of synthesizer music. It
stops.* THEO *gets up, crosses to a window and opens it. From the*
AIRSHAFT COUPLE*'s apartment, from the kitchen, we hear the
sound of a bowl falling to the floor and then spinning: wah, wah,
wah. Throughout the scene shadows are thrown of bodies moving
in the kitchen, but we can't actually see the bodies themselves.)*

MAN'S VOICE:
            Did you throw that

WOMAN'S VOICE:
            No

MAN'S VOICE:
            Oh I thought you threw it

WOMAN'S VOICE:
            It dropped

MAN'S VOICE:
            Is it broken

WOMAN'S VOICE:
            No

MAN'S VOICE:
            Oh

            (The man walks away and then returns.)

MAN'S VOICE:
            Is this yours

WOMAN'S VOICE:
> Where did you find that

MAN'S VOICE:
> On the bottom shelf

WOMAN'S VOICE:
> Which bottom shelf

MAN'S VOICE:
> The bottom shelf of the gray thing

WOMAN'S VOICE:
> Oh

MAN'S VOICE:
> I've never seen it before

WOMAN'S VOICE:
> Someone gave it to me
> I forget who

MAN'S VOICE:
> Do you want it

WOMAN'S VOICE:
> I forgot I had it

MAN'S VOICE:
> Should I get rid of it

WOMAN'S VOICE:
> No

MAN'S VOICE:
> You forgot you had it

WOMAN'S VOICE:
 I might want it

MAN'S VOICE:
 You forgot you had it but now you want it

WOMAN'S VOICE:
 I forgot I might want it

MAN'S VOICE:
 Do you forget what you might want a lot

WOMAN'S VOICE:
 Constantly

 *(FRANK knocks on THEO's door and THEO closes the
 window before answering the door.)*

FRANK: What rhymes with
         Letter of Eviction

         (FRANK hands THEO a letter.)

THEO: *(reading)*
         Uh-oh

         (SLIGHT PAUSE.)

FRANK: Is that all you have to

         (SLIGHT PAUSE.)

THEO: say

*(Apparently. BABETTE appears from the stairwell. As she distributes
the candy bars and the mouthwash it turns into a mutual exchange
as together THEO and FRANK hand BABETTE the letter.)*

BABETTE: *(reading)*
         Uh-oh

         (FRANK *looks at her expectantly.*)

BABETTE: *(that's genuine tough luck)*
         Say

                    (PAUSE.)

THEO: Let Her Love The Kitchen

                    (SLIGHT PAUSE.)

BABETTE & THEO:
         *(each saying the other's name at the end of the line, with
         emphasis)*
         I guess if you're stuck you could stay with me
         or
         Babette/Theo

                    (PAUSE.)

FRANK: I can't think about it right now

BABETTE & THEO:
         (relieved, each picking two out of three words)
         Okay/Say/Boy

              (BABETTE *unlocks her door.*)

THEO: Babette was there any change
         from the Candy Bars

BABETTE: Oh yes I forgot

              (BABETTE *hands* THEO *his change.*)

THEO: *(selective memory is a fascinating thing)*
            Oh yes I forgot I need to get back to work

BABETTE: Thrill-o-rama still

THEO: It's a complicated piece

BABETTE: The first two bars Still sound really good

THEO: Did she just Hit that adverb with something akin to
            Mockery or was that Merely my iMagination

BABETTE: I just said that Thrill-o-rama's first two
            bars Still sound really good

(BABETTE *and* THEO *enter their apartments and close the door.*
FRANK *lingers in the hallway, Little Boy Lost, holding his Letter of*
Eviction. We hear a couple of loud meows.)

(THEO *sits at his synthesizer. He stares at the keyboard. He*
is seen in shadow behind his blind. In compositional hell,
THEO *will punctuate the following section with abortive*
and puny attempts to further his score.)

(BABETTE *is standing next to a table on which rests a jar filled*
with coins; BABETTE *makes rolls of quarters, dimes, nickels, and*
pennies throughout the section. Or perhaps she has one of those
plastic coin organizer things into which one can insert a bunch of
coins and it sorts them by denomination. We should have noticed,
incidentally, that her apartment is appointed with few things.)

(FRANK *sits in a schoolhouse-type chair in his apartment; he has*
an instructional pamphlet open on his lap. A tape recorder sits
nearby. Throughout this section he is flipping through the pamphlet,
practicing different exercises and listening to his Very Important
Cassette Tape. FRANK *presses "play" on his tape recorder.)*

VERY IMPORTANT CASSETTE TAPE:
> "This training record is a part of the home study course of the Missouri Auction School, Kansas City, Missouri. Its purpose is to assist you with the various methods of bid calling, filler words, and general auction salesmanship. Auctioneering offers you a pleasant and honorable profession. The well-trained auctioneer is always in demand. You may be self-employed. Your life is enjoyable. You meet fine people. The hours are short, the pay sure."

> (FRANK *stops the tape and practices a lip trill as* BABETTE *speaks into the phone.*)

BABETTE: Larry it's me
No Me
No Me

> (LARRY *tries to escape.*)

BABETTE: I'm willing to call wait

> (BABETTE *waits as:*)

THEO: (*makes a puny attempt to further his score.*)

> (FRANK *presses "play" again.*)

VERY IMPORTANT CASSETTE TAPE:
> "Most auctioneers use two different chants. One is what we call a talking type chant that sounds like this. (*He demonstrates.*) The other is what we call more of a rhythmn chant. (*He demonstrates.*)"

(FRANK *stops the tape and rolls his r's.* LARRY *has flashed back from call waiting and voices his dubiousness about the ingenuousness of* BABETTE*'s call during her line.*)

BABETTE: Hi
          I was calling to ask
          I was calling to ask
          No I Was Not Calling To Ask You To Lend Me

(FRANK *presses "play" on his tape recorder, so that "Let's*
drill" comes in on top of BABETTE*'s "To Ask," and "One*
dollar" comes in right after BABETTE*'s "To Lend Me.")*

VERY IMPORTANT CASSETE TAPE AND FRANK:
          "Let's drill
          One dollar one dollar two dollar two dollar
          three dollar three dollar four dollar four dollar
          five dollar five dollar."

(FRANK *stops the tape in order to study a passage in the manual*
as LARRY *abruptly puts* BABETTE *on hold again.)*

BABETTE: I'm still willing to call wait

(FRANK *attempts an exercise from his manual.)*

FRANK: Course your cousin couldn't kiss you cause you can't
             kiss kin
          Course your cousin couldn't kiss you cause you can't
             kiss kin

(FRANK *repeats this exercise, faster, but at a lower volume.* LARRY
has flashed back from call waiting, although his commitment to the
conversation is truly waning. Meanwhile, during the following
THEO *makes more puny compositional attempts.)*

BABETTE: Hi
          I Was Calling To See

THEO: *(Plink.)*

BABETTE: To See

THEO: *(Plink.)*

BABETTE: To Find Out

THEO: *(Plink, plink.)*

BABETTE: if any of the Stuff I
         brought in last week has Sold

   (FRANK *fantasizes about a sale, perfecting his technique.*)

FRANK: *(says first "sold" with Babette's "sold")*
          Sold *(gavel sound)* Sold *(gavel sound)* Sold *(gavel sound)*

BABETTE: that's all
         since
         my book is This Close To Completion
         My book
         My book
         Larry you can't tell me in all seriousness that I haven't
         told you about
         My Book

   (*Barely concealed laughter coupled with an attempt to extricate
      himself from conversation on* LARRY's *part.*)

BABETTE: Uh huh well you're in luck as
         I'm more than willing to call wait

THEO: *(thinks he's inspired but is sadly mistaken.)*

             (FRANK *presses "play."*)

VERY IMPORTANT CASSETTE TAPE:
         "Back to the business of polishing up that all-impor-
         tant chant, the sound that moves millions—I mean
         people and dollars. And it's a curious fact that auc-

tioneers bear the honorary title of colonel. It dates
back to the days just after the Civil War when army
colonels handled the job of disposing of cannon,
guns, mules, and other military equipment, all at pub-
lic auction."

(FRANK presses "stop" as Larry oh-so-reluctantly returns.)

BABETTE: Hi
So I'm trying to Buy Some Time
so
Well has the fur vase sold I know there was
water damage but
and the glow-in-the-dark telephone table
What about the lamp covered with those
charming depictions of mid-century coal mining
agitation Well
are you sure you've displayed it Prominently Enough
oh can you call wait a second

THEO: *(makes yet another pathetically puny attempt.)*

(BABETTE flashes to call waiting.)

BABETTE: Hello
Who's calling
No Babette moved
No far
I'm pretty sure she died actually and
her debts died with her
That's what I heard anyway Sorry

(BABETTE flashes back to LARRY.)

BABETTE: Sorry so
Larry
Larry
Larry

(BABETTE *paces a little and then redials as:*)

THEO: (*'s plinks become plonks.*)

BABETTE: Larry Me

(FRANK *presses "play" once again, as, throughout the following,*
BABETTE *listens to* LARRY*'s unbridled outburst, the content of*
which we cannot make out, the volume of which perhaps we can.)

VERY IMPORTANT CASSETTE TAPE:
        "For well over half a century many of America's fore-
        most auctioneers have obtained their initial training
        in Kansas City. A sincere welcome awaits you here in
        Kansas City, and every effort will be made to make this
        the most pleasant and profitable two weeks of your
        lifetime."

(FRANK *stops the tape as* BABETTE *hangs up the phone in frus-*
tration and then yells in its direction, in response to LARRY:)

BABETTE Phone calls are Self-Serving by DEFINITION
        and BEsides
        It's All For The Sake Of MY BOOK

THEO: (*accuses his synthesizer with Germanic non-words of*
        disgust.)

(FRANK *crosses to his window and opens it. In the* AIR-
SHAFT COUPLE*'s apartment the woman, who's in the*
kitchen, calls to the man, who's in the bedroom.)

WOMAN'S VOICE:
        I'm making toast

(*No response.*)

WOMAN'S VOICE:
    I'm making toast

            (No response.)

WOMAN'S VOICE:
    I'm making toast

            (No response.)

*(A set of keys is thrown into the kitchen from the
bedroom. It hits the floor.)*

MAN'S VOICE:
    Before I forget

*(Sound of the woman stepping down off a stool and picking
up the set of keys from the floor. The woman clears her
throat. The following is overlapped conversation. Each new
line begins at the "/" of the previous line.)*

WOMAN'S VOICE:
    Did you call the bank guy/ about the account

MAN'S VOICE:
    He says we have to go/ in

WOMAN's VOICE:
    Why do we have/ to go in

MAN'S VOICE:
    To sign/ something

WOMAN'S VOICE:
    We can't just do it over/ the phone

MAN'S VOICE:
    I said we have to sign/ something

WOMAN'S VOICE:
When should we/ go in

MAN'S VOICE:
We don't have to go in/ together

WOMAN'S VOICE:
We/ don't Oh Okay Well that's different

MAN'S VOICE:
We just have to sign it You can sign it and I'll sign it We
don't have to sign it together we just both have to sign
it We can't just do it over the phone

(Sound of the woman buttering toast.)

WOMAN'S VOICE:
You must be hungry

(Toast is thrown from the kitchen into the bedroom.)

THE EXPOSITION SCENE

(BABETTE, FRANK, *and* THEO)

BABETTE: Before I knew Frank Larry told me he was saving up
money to be Frozen

THEO: I'd heard from Larry that this girl
Babette this woman was an editor who specialized in
incredibly obscure subject matter which I understood to
mean that she was mostly out of work

BABETTE: It took a month or two before I understood that it was some
guy Theo who was saving up to be Frozen not
some guy Frank

FRANK: Larry said something about some guy
having lost his wife
literally

THEO: Larry told me that he'd been seeing some guy named Frank for
a while but that things were going Disastrously

FRANK: I asked Larry what do you mean he lost his wife Did she die
Did he leave her somewhere Were they at a
Mall

THEO: Larry's pretty unlucky in love but
This Guy Frank sounded particularly awful

FRANK: Larry and I were doing Really Well at that point except
I wondered about his friends who to a
one sounded like a bunch of Losers

BABETTE: I was worried about Larry seeing a guy who sounded like such
a Loser I mean a Profound Loser Profoundly Depressed
and in Profound Denial
Larry also told me that the guy who was saving up to be
Frozen also lost his wife
What do you mean Lost His Wife
At the Mall or something

THEO: I started to get this paranoid
feeling that Larry was telling everybody my
personal business

FRANK: Besides the guy who Lost His Wife At The Mall Larry
           also talked about this woman named Babette this
           unemployed faux literary person who was always
               borrowing
           money from him and
           never repaying him and how he found it impossible
               to say no
           to her even though he had absolutely no desire to
               sleep with
           her which was good because he was sleeping with me
               but
           it became a point of curiosity for me because Why Lend
           Money To Someone You Aren't Interested In Sleeping
               With

BABETTE: Then one day I bumped into Theo at Larry's Shop and
               Larry
           introduced us
           I asked him if it was true that he was saving up to be
           frozen and with bug-esque eyes full of accusation
               and hurt
           he looked
           over at Larry and then back at me and hissed None Of
               Your
           Beeswax
           He also said he was saving up to buy a really ancient
               bonsai
           plant

THEO: Tree

BABETTE: but I could tell that part was a lie an arcane and
               fictitious addition to his autobiography designed to
                   deflect
               attention from the Truly Strange Fact
               that He Was Actually Saving Up To Be Frozen

THEO: One day when Larry had invited me over to the store he
          suddenly ran into the back and said to say that he
          Wasn't In this Woman came in and started to waltz
          into the back and I said Excuse Me
          Larry's
          Not
          In and she
          said Who Might You Be and I said I'm Theo I'm Sure
              and she
          asked me Rather Aggressively if I was the one who was
              saving
          up to be Frozen
          and she hit that word Frozen with an industrial mallet
              full
          of judgment and preconception
          and I tried to pretend I hadn't heard the question but
          she said No Really Are You and I said very calmly
              you know
          and with a smile in my voice I said None Of Your
              Beeswax

BABETTE: Just hissed it None Of Your Beeswax

THEO: And are You The One Who's Sending Larry To The
          Poor House
          You Must Be Babette Yes He's Told Me About You

FRANK: Finally I ran into Both Of Them One
          day when I
          stopped by the store as a Special Surprise
          For Larry and there
          They Both Were sharing what seemed to be a rather
          Charged Silence and I started
          to walk into the back and they said in unison
          Larry's Not In
          and I kept walking because Larry Was Always In For
          Me

BABETTE: Larry called out to me from the back suddenly

THEO: Larry dropped something in the back suddenly

FRANK: Larry emerged from the back suddenly and put his
          arm around me and said
          Frank this is Theo this is Babette I've
          So Longed For Them To Meet You

BABETTE: and said Babette These Are The Two I've
          Been Telling You About

THEO: and said Theo I Asked You To Do One Thing

BABETTE: They weren't at all what I expected

THEO: They weren't at all what I expected

FRANK: They were exactly what I expected

                    (SLIGHT PAUSE.)

FRANK: I don't exactly know how we became friends but it was
          some time after
          Larry told me I wasn't the guy for him

THEO: I didn't like either one of them at first but then one of
          them sublet their way into my building and then
          the other got the other an
          apartment and somehow we were all
          neighbors and when you share a landlord with people
          you have
          of course a
          Built-In Common Enemy and there's just about noth-
          ing more
          bond-inducing than Sharply Focused Ill Will

BABETTE: Basically I think we all felt a little
                  sorry for each other Isn't that how most friendships
                  start I mean when
                  choosing friends you're either drawn to people You
                  Wish You Were or you're drawn to
                  people You're Afraid You Are

(THEO *sits at his synthesizer, while* BABETTE *and*
FRANK *stand in his open doorway.*)

THEO: It's not finished but its main themes are in place

(THEO *prepares to play as if he were giving a concert at
Carnegie Hall. He plays for a very short time, then looks expectantly toward the door, toward his friends. The development in
the piece of music is virtually indiscernible.*)

(*We hear the sound of the throaty-voiced very old
woman having a good laugh.*)

VOICE OF MRS. JORGENSON:
                  Alas Alas

END OF PART I

PART II

(BABETTE, THEO, *and* FRANK *stand in the hallway.*)

THEO: That's so odd

FRANK: You never know

BABETTE: It makes me want to move

THEO: Everything makes you want to move

BABETTE: Maybe because I want to move Is she still there

THEO: Of course not

FRANK: Yes

BABETTE & THEO:
           Ew

BABETTE: When did it happen

THEO: Frank said Weren't you listening Late last night

FRANK: Early this morning

BABETTE: Exactly I mean
           I wonder if I had a parallel dream

FRANK: No one knows I found her at ten by which point she
         seemed let's say deeply invested in her death

BABETTE & THEO:
         Wow

THEO: I'm glad it was you I wouldn't have known who to call

FRANK: I haven't called anyone

THEO & BABETTE:
         You haven't

FRANK: What's the rush

THEO: I guess you're right

BABETTE: Does she have family

FRANK: She never mentioned family to me

BABETTE: She never mentioned family to me

THEO: She mentioned family to me

FRANK & BABETTE:
         Likc what

THEO: Children but I think they were estranged

BABETTE: Oh yeah the estranged children that's right

FRANK: Oh yeah well I knew about the estranged children
         I thought we were talking about active familial relations

THEO: I think we should call someone

FRANK: But I've been thinking

BABETTE: I've had parallel dreams before you know I've been
              known to
            be uncannily in tune with calamitous events

THEO: I'll say Jane

BABETTE: *(to Theo)*
            What was that

THEO: I didn't hear anything

FRANK: I found a note

BABETTE: You kept it

THEO: Shouldn't you have

FRANK: Do you want to see it

BABETTE & THEO:
            Yes

(FRANK *pulls a piece of paper out of his pocket.* THEO *and*
BABETTE *try to read it for themselves, but* FRANK *holds the note
        close to his chest and reads out loud.)*

FRANK: See ya

BABETTE & THEO:
            Wow

BABETTE: Concise

FRANK: Mm hmm

THEO: Do we know anyone who needs an apartment

(THEO *and* BABETTE *put their fingers on their chins for a moment and shift their eyes in unison.* FRANK *regards them expectantly.*)

BABETTE: What's the exact layout again

THEO: Is it nicer than mine

BABETTE: I think it's bigger than mine but I think it's
          darker than mine

THEO: And no doubt cheaper than mine

BABETTE: And no doubt quieter than mine

FRANK: Uh I need an apartment

THEO & BABETTE:
          (each picks two out of three)
          Oh that's right/Of course/Yes you do

FRANK: They'll do a cosmetic fix-up and jack up the rent They
          can do that

THEO & BABETTE:
          You're right they can

FRANK: That's what they do

THEO & BABETTE:
          You're right it is

                    (SLIGHT PAUSE.)

BABETTE: Hey listen do you want to see the snapshots from that
          trip I took last year

(FRANK *and* THEO *eye each other as* BABETTE *pulls
them out of her coat pocket.*)

THEO & FRANK:
          (unsure)
          Sure

FRANK: I thought they were holding those hostage

BABETTE: They were but they finally threw them out today and my
          little friend at the Quick Clicks tipped me off

THEO: What exactly is a little friend

                    (BABETTE *opens the packet.*)

BABETTE: Wait a minute This
          isn't my trip They must've mixed up names at the
          Quick Clicks

THEO & FRANK:
          (suddenly more interested)
          Let's see

          (ALL THREE *crowd around the photos.*)

ALL THREE:
          Wow it's
          Mrs. Jorgenson

FRANK: Who's the guy

THEO: What are they

          (BABETTE *and* FRANK *look at* THEO *in unison, then
          turn back to the photograph.*)

BABETTE: He looks young In terms of what we can see

FRANK: I should probably hold on to these They should prob-
           ably stay with the note

THEO: Or I could keep them since I have better locks

BABETTE: They're mine you perverts they're mine
           but
           I wonder who's flipping through my trip

FRANK: It looks like Mrs. Jorgenson's trip was more eventful

BABETTE: How do you know

THEO: What do you mean by that Babette

BABETTE: My life is full of
           events

THEO & FRANK:
           (hurt/surprised, i.e., Theo is hurt, Frank surprised)
           Really

THEO: You don't think this guy did something to Mrs.
           Jorgenson

BABETTE & FRANK:
           (annoyed/philosophical)
           You saw the pictures Theo he obviously did something
               to Mrs.
           Jorgenson

THEO: No I mean in terms of foul play

BABETTE & FRANK:
           (annoyed/philosophical)
           Depends on your definition

THEO: In terms of her death did it look like she met with foul
           play

FRANK: It looked like she was sleeping It probably still does

BABETTE: Why are you using that language Met with foul play
              What is
           that exactly

THEO: An uh expression

BABETTE: *(everything about him is annoying)*
           How do you do that with your eyebrow

THEO: It's involuntary but I'm glad you find it compelling

BABETTE: I didn't say that

FRANK: What's wrong with you

THEO & BABETTE:
           Nothing

FRANK: I meant Babette

THEO: Oh
           Listen I have to make a call

BABETTE: See ya
           I mean

FRANK: Bye Theo

THEO: Are you two staying out here

FRANK: I don't know

BABETTE: Why Theo

THEO: Maybe I'll wait to make that call

BABETTE: Actually I have to clean my apartment

FRANK: My cats are probably hungry

(FRANK *and* BABETTE *unlock their doors.* THEO *follows suit. As soon as* FRANK *enters his apartment and the door starts to close* THEO *addresses* BABETTE *just before her door shuts.*)

THEO: Can I talk to you Babette

BABETTE: Is it about Mrs. Jorgenson

THEO: As a matter of fact it's not about Mrs. Jorgenson It's about what happened between us last week

BABETTE: I thought

THEO: We did I just had One More Quick Question

BABETTE: It's not that much fun to talk about this

THEO: When I started doing that thing you know right before you

(FRANK*'s door opens.*)

FRANK: I thought I heard voices

BABETTE: Theo can't stop thinking about Mrs. Jorgenson

FRANK: Who can

(SLIGHT PAUSE.)

THEO: Okay

ALL THREE:
           See ya
           around

(ALL THREE *enter their respective apartments and
           almost close their doors.*)

FRANK: Has anyone heard from Larry

THEO & BABETTE:
           Depends on your definition of heard

FRANK: Uh Have either of you spoken to him

THEO & BABETTE:
           (each picks two out of three)
           Briefly/In passing/Just hi bye

FRANK: Is he okay

THEO & BABETTE:
           (each picks two out of three)
           Seems it/Fine/Far as I can tell

BABETTE: Oh boy Look at the time You have to run Theo

FRANK: Say hi to Dr. Greenspan

THEO: Okay will do When do you see her next Babette

BABETTE: I can't afford mental illness right now

FRANK: You'd better hurry Theo Otherwise you'll have to waste
            precious time talking about why you Chose To
            Be Late

THEO: I guess you're right I'll see you guys later
            Right

FRANK & BABETTE:
            (each says one)
            Bye/Right

            (THEO *exits down the stairs.*)

BABETTE: Frank I need to talk to you

FRANK: Is it about the annoying manner in which Theo's
            approaching
            life these days

BABETTE: As a matter of fact it's not about the annoying manner in
            which Theo's approaching life these days It's about

FRANK & BABETTE:
            Mrs. Jorgenson

BABETTE: She pulled me aside recently
            and mentioned something that I find
            in retrospect quite disturbing

FRANK: I think I know what you're
            going to say That you think that
            I had something against Mrs.
            Jorgenson

BABETTE: She did say something to that
            effect I brushed it off Frank
            I assure you at the time

FRANK: She played loud music Babette
             At all hours She was constantly
             reciting poetry in that remarkable late octogenarian
                 chain-
             smoking tenor voice of hers But she didn't
             recite the good modern ones she Nooooooo
             she didn't have the decency Mostly
             she picked that old windbag Whitman
             I'm sorry I know it's sacrilege to say but

BABETTE: Frank you misunderstand Mrs. Jorgenson told me she
                 was in
             love with you I guess the Whitman was just an attention
             getting ploy

FRANK: Oh brother

BABETTE: Did you and Mrs. Jorgenson
             How should I put this

FRANK: She wasn't my gender as you know
             although she had great ankles and wrists They
                 usually are
             attractive in sync I find Anyway I had a thought that
             happens to involve

FRANK & BABETTE:
             (statement/question)
             Mrs. Jorgenson

             (THEO appears in the hallway.)

THEO: I
             forgot something

FRANK: We were just talking about how great it would be if we
                 all
             went to the beach

THEO: A day at the beach Great idea

BABETTE: I HATE THE BEACH

    (BABETTE *slams her door.*)

THEO: What's eating her

FRANK: I didn't say anything to upset her if that's what you mean

THEO: Did you just hit that personal pronoun or was that my imagination

FRANK: I just said that I didn't say anything to upset her

THEO: There You did it again

FRANK: Did you really forget something
Theo or were you just inventing an
excuse to return to see if Babette and
I were having a private conversation

THEO: Do you think it's possible that Babette's out of love
    with
love

FRANK: Anything's possible

    (*We hear a couple of loud meows.*)

FRANK: I still haven't fed them

    (FRANK *turns to enter his apartment.*)

THEO: Frank I think you should know
           that something's going on between
           Babette and me although we would
           never let that come between our
           friendship with you

                    (BABETTE's *door flings open.*)

BABETTE: What are you saying lunatic There's
           nothing going on Frank

                    (BABETTE's *door slams shut.*)

THEO: Frank

FRANK: I'VE GOT TO BE A RESPONSIBLE PET
           OWNER THEO PLEASE

                    (FRANK *enters his apartment.*)

                    (BABETTE's *door opens a crack.*)

BABETTE: How dare you Theo

THEO: We're close friends He has a right
           to know if you and I are seeing each other

BABETTE: I don't even remember the incident Theo
           Recall that I was drunk
           Go get graced by the gift of retrospect

              (BABETTE's *door starts to close, but* THEO *jams his
              foot in it to prevent it from closing all the way.*)

THEO: You'll see

BABETTE: LISTEN I'm not going to be pushed into a situation
            with you
            where every time I see you the embrace is awkward
            and
            neither Fish Nor
            Fowl It's hard enough to hug as it is

(BABETTE *slams her door.* THEO *walks toward the stairwell.*)

(BABETTE *is standing in her apartment. She is situated behind her window shade, so that all we see of her is
her shadow. She is on the phone.*)

BABETTE: (*a torrent of words with line breaks*)
            It was on a subway train I was
            headed uptown and I
            sat down next to a Strange Old Lady who was reading
                a book
            the
            title of which I couldn't see I happened to
            sit down right at the beginning of a
            chapter She was roughly a third of the way through
                the book
            Anyway
            I of course having forgotten to bring reading
            material of my own started
            reading the book over her Strange Old Lady
                Shoulder and
            became immediately absorbed in the story Each
            time we reached a station I
            tensed in fear that the Strange
            Old Lady would get off the train and leave me
            hanging but she didn't get off the train She didn't
            leave me We
            seemed to read at exactly the same speed She
            turned the pages with an uncanny timing that seemed
            based purely on the speed with which I was reading
                until at

some point I'd reached the end of the
page and the page didn't
turn I
waited for Several Seconds Then a minute Then two full
minutes Then finally I looked over at the
Strange Old Lady and saw that she'd
fallen asleep This was very distressing because I was very
absorbed and I really wanted to know what happened
next so I turned the page I turned the page and
     read the
next two pages and then turned the page again and again
until I'd read another
oh
ten pages and then the Strange Old Lady woke up and she
started to read again and she
paused and she
turned back to the page before and then she
turned back to the page before that and so on until
     without
looking up she said
Can you hang on a second

(BABETTE *has raised her blind and has been struggling to open*
her window during the last part of her speech. She places the
receiver on her windowsill and expends a considerable amount of
energy forcing her window open. Finally she succeeds, but before
she re-engages in her telephone conversation she becomes distracted
by the conversation occurring between the AIRSHAFT COUPLE,
who are in offstage, but separate, rooms. As they speak, they each
sort through a pile of books and place them just inside the stage
area, so that only their hands, parts of their arms, and the books
themselves are visible to the audience. The sound of books stacked
upon one another adds a percussive note to the scene.)

MAN'S VOICE:
     Yours

WOMAN'S VOICE:
Yours

MAN'S VOICE:
Yours

WOMAN'S VOICE:
Yours

MAN'S VOICE:
Mine

WOMAN'S VOICE:
Yours

MAN'S VOICE:
Mine

WOMAN'S VOICE:
Yours

MAN'S VOICE:
Mine

WOMAN'S VOICE:
Mine

MAN'S VOICE:
Mine

WOMAN'S VOICE:
Mine

MAN'S VOICE:
Mine

WOMAN'S VOICE:
Mine

MAN'S VOICE:
> Mine

WOMAN'S VOICE:
> Mine

MAN'S VOICE:
> Yours

WOMAN'S VOICE:
> Yours

MAN'S VOICE:
> Mine

WOMAN'S VOICE:
> Mine

MAN'S VOICE:
> Are you saying you no longer like the way I look

WOMAN'S VOICE:
> I'm saying I no longer like the way I look at you

MAN'S VOICE:
> Yours

WOMAN'S VOICE:
> Mine

MAN'S VOICE:
> Yours

WOMAN'S VOICE:
> Mine

MAN'S VOICE:
  Yours

  (BABETTE *remembers her telephone conversation and picks*
  up receiver from the sill. Perhaps the rest of BABETTE*'s*
  monologue is scored by a slightly muted continuation of the
  AIRSHAFT COUPLE*'s book-sorting dialogue: "Yours,"*
  "Mine," but mostly "Mine"'s.)

BABETTE: Sorry so the Strange Old Lady turned those
  military-blue eyes on me and said
  So What's The Story
  and I mumbled something about having turned
  several pages and the Strange Old Lady cut me off and
   said
  No Whadd'I Miss
  And I said Oh In The Story
  And I said Annabelle
  And the Strange Old Lady corrected me and said
   Isabelle
  And I said sorry Isabelle made it to the other side
  And the Strange Old Lady said that's impossible
  And I said it's not impossible if Isabelle fashioned
   some
  kind of raft
  And she said
  Out of what
  And I said
  Out of wood
  And she said
  There are no trees on the island We learned that chapters
  ago
  And I said
  I came in late
  And she said
  Isabelle must've hitched a ride on someone else's raft
  And I said
  Whose raft

And she said
A native must've been passing by
And I said
Native of where
And she said
Oh   spare   me   your   Knee-jerk   Literal-minded
    Bourgeois World-
view would ya It's a Gee Dee romance novel For
    Crying Out
Loud
And I said
Aren't you being literal-minded about the trees
And she said
That's different That's internal logic
And I said
I am not bourgeois
And she said
Did Isabelle reach Karl with the antidote
And I said
Not yet and the vial is leaking and
I am not bourgeois
And she said
If you can spell bourgeois you're bourgeois
And then the Strange Old Lady grabbed me by the
    arm and
whispered in my ear in that
oddly elegant Bronx-soaked Camel Light croak of hers
Meet Me At Three On The Downtown Train
and she was gone
and I did
and we read until Karl uttered his Last Words
which were
Alas Alas

(On second thought:)

Actually that's not
true Karl said
Alack Alack
Alas implies pity whereas Alack says regret
Karl said Alack and that's
the first memory I have of Mrs. Jorgenson Llllisten
My Book is This Close To Completion and
I was wondering if by any chance you
could ssssspare
Okay Okay Understood
Okay
'kay
'kay
'kay

(BABETTE *hangs up the phone.*)

I am not bourgeois

(Momentary silence that is broken by the AIRSHAFT COUPLE:)

MAN'S VOICE:
I'm still hungry

WOMAN'S VOICE:
Call for something

MAN'S VOICE:
What do you feel like

WOMAN'S VOICE:
I don't care

MAN'S VOICE:
You don't care what you feel like
or you don't
care what I call for

WOMAN'S VOICE:
    Both no
    the last thing

MAN'S VOICE:
    In other words you don't want to make

WOMAN'S VOICE:
    Right right

MAN'S VOICE:
    So what
    Chinese

WOMAN'S VOICE:
    But
    nothing too eggy

MAN'S VOICE:
    Eggy

WOMAN'S VOICE:
    Eggy Eggy Eggy Eggy Eggy

(THEO is sitting in a chair that is suspended in the air.)

THEO: She has a tendency to deny what is right
    in front of her I try to point out to her what's going on
    the reality of the case but I suppose certain of her
    defense mechanisms kick in and do her a disservice
    I've tried to be patient I've waited it out all these
    years now you know but just as I get a littlesatisfaction
    in terms of physical contact not that other types of contact
    aren't important I value our friendship of course she pulls
    away and as I said tries to deny what we both know to be
    true that we have fallen deeply in love with one
        another and
    should probably marry the sooner the better

VOICE OF DR. GREENSPAN:
    Is it possible that you've
    misread the situation

THEO: No absolutely not No it's not possible The facts have been
    staring both of us all of us right in the face No No No

VOICE OF DR. GREENSPAN:
    Go on

THEO: No

VOICE OF DR. GREENSPAN:
    We're running out of time Theo

THEO: You'll see

*(We hear the sound of the same piece of synthesizer
music.* BABETTE *emerges from her apartment and
knocks on* FRANK'*s door. He answers it.)*

BABETTE: Hungry

FRANK: I guess

BABETTE: Why not order something

FRANK: All right Any ideas

BABETTE: Moo Shoo Easy on the egg tell them

FRANK: Anything else

BABETTE: Anything preceded by General That's always
    good And egg rolls And whatever You want

FRANK: Okay

(FRANK *closes his door as* THEO *appears in the hallway.*
BABETTE *sees him and starts to enter her apartment.*)

THEO: You can run

BABETTE: I'm not hiding Theo

THEO: Why don't you come over I'll give you a
           massage and we'll talk this Thing through

BABETTE: You say Thing Theo like it has a capital letter and it
           doesn't have a capital letter Theo There's no thing in
           the
           Thing Theo and Theo I think you need to give Susan
               what's-
           her-name with the hair a call

THEO: You're lying that's not
           what you really
           think

BABETTE: Oh really Tell me what I
           Really Think

THEO: You wish external circumstances would mirror internal
           circumstances
           You wonder why our fateful encounter did not occur
               sooner
           You want me

BABETTE: I wish you'd recall that I was

BABETTE & THEO:
           drunk

BABETTE: I wonder when you became this tiresome
I want you
to leave me the four letters sounds like duck alone

THEO: Poor deluded Babette

(FRANK's *door opens.*)

FRANK: They didn't have anything General so I
ordered something Chairman

BABETTE: As long as the chicken's authoritative

FRANK: Are you joining us for dinner

THEO: Okay

(BABETTE *enters her apartment and slams the door.*)

SEVERAL PSEUDO SCENES OF LOVE
THWARTED AT EVERY TURN

FRANK: Listen Theo do you have a minute

THEO: Is it about Babette

FRANK: As a matter of fact it's not about Babette It's about the
erotic dreams I've recently been having
in which you figure prominently

THEO: I'm flattered Frank but I'm afraid
your dreams won't do me any good
I'd better check my machine before
dinner She's probably called

(THEO *enters his apartment as* BABETTE *emerges from hers.*)

BABETTE: Whatever he said he's lying

FRANK: Is that what you think

BABETTE: Recall that I was

FRANK: Oddly we weren't discussing you

BABETTE: Oh
                Listen Frank I don't know why this image has floated
                      into my
                mind but do you remember that time during the
                      snowstorm when
                you
                and I were forced to

(The buzzer sounds in FRANK*'s apartment. He leans inside.)*

FRANK: Yes

VOICE OF DELIVERY PERSON: Chinese food

FRANK: Third floor
                I have to get my wallet Do You need to get Your wallet
                Babette

*(*FRANK *enters his apartment as* THEO *exits his.)*

THEO: Was that Frank's buzzer

BABETTE: The food's arrived I'd
                better get my wallet

THEO: I'll spring for you

BABETTE: We're not a couple Theo

THEO: You'll see

(BABETTE enters her apartment as FRANK exits from his. FRANK approaches the stairwell and meets the delivery person out of sight.)

FRANK: How much do We owe you

VOICE OF DELIVERY PERSON:
Twenty-five fifty-nine

FRANK: Tweny-five tweny-five tweny-five
tweny-five fitty fitty fitty fitty fitty

VOICE OF DELIVERY PERSON:
Nine

FRANK: Here you are my good man

(FRANK carries the food down the hall.)

THEO: I'll pay for Babette and me

(BABETTE emerges from her apartment.)

BABETTE: No you won't but I can't find my
wallet Frank Could you cover my part

FRANK: Sure Babette But

BABETTE: I know Frank that I owe you from not too long ago

FRANK: And not too long Babette before that

BABETTE: I don't know where Frank I left my
wallet Maybe at Larry's Shop I'm not sure

THEO: I'm buying you dinner Babette

James Urbaniak (left) as Frank, Dominic Fumusa as Theo, and Christina Kirk as Babette in the Soho Rep production of [*sic*].

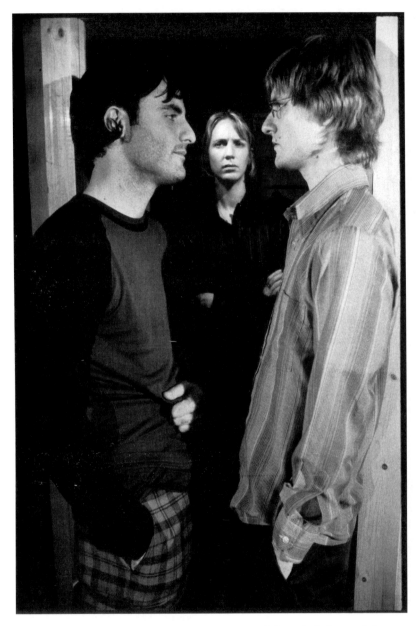

Dominic Fumusa, Christina Kirk, and James Urbaniak (left to right).

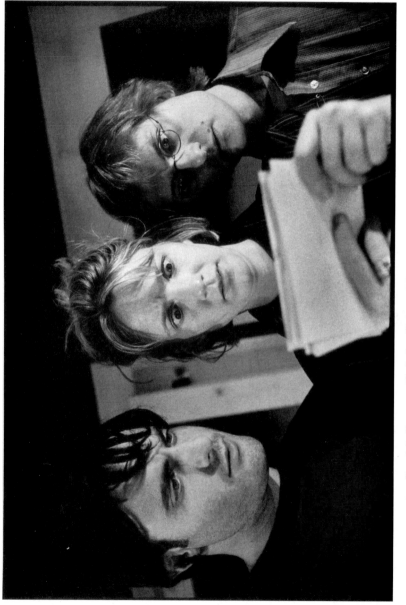

Dominic Fumusa, Christina Kirk, and James Urbaniak (left to right).

Christina Kirk, James Urbaniak, and Dominic Fumusa (left to right).
All photographs of the Soho Rep production of [*sic*] by Paula Court.

FRANK: I hope Babette you didn't leave your wallet at Larry's
            Store
            If you did you'll probably never see it again Still you
            should probably call Or I will If You Want

THEO: I'm paying for your dinner Babette That's
            final

BABETTE: Frank please lend me the money It
            won't happen again I'll call Larry right
            after dinner

FRANK: Or I mean I'll Call If You Insist

            (FRANK *has reached into the delivery bag and begun
            eating an egg roll.* THEO *also helps himself to one.*)

THEO: I SAID IT'S MY GODDAMN TREAT
            I just need to get my wallet

            (THEO *enters his apartment.*)

FRANK: Good egg rolls

BABETTE: Were they

FRANK: Oh didn't you get one

BABETTE: That's okay

            (THEO *emerges from his apartment.*)

THEO: Here you are my good man

BABETTE: When did you start saying my good man

THEO: I heard Frank say it to the delivery person

BABETTE: When did you start saying my good man

FRANK: I never stopped

(THEO *has opened up one of the main dishes and is digging in.*)

THEO: Chairman Cho's chicken I love
         Chairman Cho's chicken
         I love all communist chicken

FRANK: Larry loves communist chicken

BABETTE/THEO:
         (Oh no/not again)
         Does he/Really

FRANK: I ran into someone who saw him the other day who
              said he
         looked tired

BABETTE: Hey did I tell you that he's got one of Mrs. Jorgenson's
         paintings on the wall

FRANK: Mrs. Jorgenson couldn't paint to save her life

BABETTE & THEO:
         Guess not

THEO & BABETTE & FRANK:
         Mrs. Jorgenson

BABETTE: I think we should call someone

FRANK: I've been thinking you know

THEO: The police I guess or at least the operator

FRANK: that Mrs. Jorgenson's lease hasn't lapsed and I've been
            thinking

BABETTE & THEO:
            What are you suggesting Not what I think you're
                suggesting I
            hope Illegally appropriating Mrs. J's apartment
                because
            you've been evicted from yours Frank how could you

            (By now the Chinese food is almost gone. THEO *and*
            FRANK *are eating with their hands.)*

                        (SLIGHTEST PAUSE.)

FRANK: *(you both misunderstand)*
            I've been thinking Great moo shoo

BABETTE: Was it

THEO & FRANK:
            Oh didn't you get any

BABETTE: *(it's not fine)*
            It's fine

FRANK: I was also thinking about going out for a beer tonight
                Want
            to come along Theo

THEO: I don't think so

BABETTE: Why didn't you ask me

FRANK: Are you sure

THEO: I'm kind of tired

BABETTE: I'm not I'm not tired

FRANK: You can't find your wallet

THEO: Would you like me to take you
          out for a drink tonight Babette

BABETTE: No

FRANK: Why do you want to go all of a sudden

THEO: I'm trying to learn to respond to
          Babette's needs

BABETTE: An interesting development

FRANK: I have needs too Theo

THEO: No one's denying that I just feel tonight
          a need to be with the one I

FRANK: When did I turn into the third wheel

BABETTE: I have needs too Frank

FRANK: I think I hear my phone ringing

          (FRANK *enters his apartment suddenly.*)

BABETTE: I think I hear my phone ringing

THEO: Your phone's not ringing Babette

BABETTE: Oh but it is

(BABETTE *rushes into her apartment and* THEO *is left with the
take-out food remains, which he carries into his apartment.*)

(THEO, BABETTE, *and* FRANK *are lying in bed in
their respective apartments.* THEO *and* FRANK *are
asleep.* BABETTE *is making animal and other shadows
with her hands—rather elaborate and impressive.*)

BABETTE: I once met a man at a party as we were both going
for the same Potato Chip
Our respective hands halted
their downward descent and instead
gestured for the other to Dig In
to said Potato Chip
It became a showdown of manners We
held our hands like that for
nineteen full minutes until
finally he lifted the Potato Chip
and placed it gently on my
tongue

(BABETTE *falls asleep as* THEO *begins making
interesting animal and other shadows.*)

THEO: I worked at a skating rink as a teenager
I got to skate for free all through high school
My life pretty much continued on that rhapsodic
trajectory
right up until The Mysterious Disappearance Of My
Wife

(THEO *goes back to sleep and* FRANK *begins to make shadows.*)

FRANK: Be on the lookout for strange spots in
otherwise uniformly colored food That's
my best advice

(FRANK *goes back to sleep and* BABETTE *makes shadows again.*)

BABETTE: I once spilled red wine on a dear friend's white
carpet and nothing was ever the same

(BABETTE *goes back to sleep as* THEO *makes shadows again.*)

THEO: Maybe I never gave her my last piece of gum

(THEO *goes back to sleep as* FRANK *makes shadows again.*)

FRANK: People talk about things they know nothing about all
                  the
           time
           and with confidence
           and with nerve

(FRANK *goes back to sleep as* BABETTE *makes shadows again.*)

BABETTE: If someone asks you if you're free on the weekend they
           Might want to take you to brunch but they Probably
           want you to help them move

           (BABETTE *continues to make shadows as* THEO
              wakes up and also makes shadows.)

THEO: And though good things have happened and though I've
           assembled some very complicated model airplanes
                  over the
           years my disappearing wife will not reappear I
           know that for a strong feeling

           (FRANK *wakes up and joins the other two in making
              shadows. He practices lip trills briefly.*)

FRANK: The question is why must I
           spend my life assessing the
           pregnancy of any given
           pause

BABETTE: Who are these people who come unexpectedly into small
fortunes That's what I'd like to know

THEO: In lieu of living life with my wife
I suppose I would like to end up with
someone with a fondness for remaining

FRANK: Please pardon my partially purple paisley pants
Please pardon my partially purple paisley pants
Please pardon my partially purple paisley pants

(SLIGHT PAUSE.)

FRANK: Basically I guess I'd just like to
wind up with someone who'd say after
I'd walked through the front door
boy am I glad to see you

THEO: *(starts speaking after Frank says "after")*
Basically I guess I'd just like to
wind up with someone who'd say after
I'd walked through the front door
boy am I glad to see you

BABETTE: *(starts speaking after Theo says "after")*
Basically I guess I'd just like to
wind up with someone who'd say after
I'd walked through the front door
boy am I glad to see you

*(The hallway, a few moments later. FRANK has his
hand on the doorknob of Mrs. Jorgenson's door as
BABETTE and THEO emerge from their apartments.)*

BABETTE: *(are you doing)*
What

THEO: *('s going on)*
           What

FRANK: *(did I do)*
           What

END OF PART II

PART III

(FRANK, BABETTE and THEO are in their own apartments. THEO is seated at his synthesizer which, according to him, is clearly malfunctioning; he spends the scene attempting to repair it. BABETTE is on the phone, and FRANK is standing, holding his tape recorder in the palms of his hands at chest level. FRANK presses "play.")

VERY IMPORTANT CASSETTE TAPE:
"You practice it when you're driving down the road, you practice it when you're going in the shower, this morning, in the morning, tonight, wherever you are I want you to practice it and practice breathin' right."

(FRANK stops the tape.)

BABETTE: *(on the phone)*
It's actually a compendium of mostly twentieth century outburst

(FRANK presses "play.")

VERY IMPORTANT CASSETTE TAPE:
"Eight hundred dollar bid and now fifty
Now go on! You didn't take that big deep breath to start with! Before you start it, get a good deep breath and then go!"

BABETTE: Twentieth
          Century
          Outburst

VERY IMPORTANT CASSETTE TAPE:
          "Eight hundred dollar bid and now fifty now fifty
          Bid
          Eight fifty bid and now nine now nine nine bid will
               you give me nine
          Bid nine
          Nine hundred dollar bid and now fifty
          Bid
          Nine hundred dollar bid and now fifty now fifty will
               you give me fifty"

               (FRANK *stops the tape.*)

BABETTE: Little-known stuff
          Outbursts by Unknowns
          that had repercussions of a uh
          Global Nature

(FRANK *presses "play" on the tape recorder. Note: as* FRANK
*attempts to practice the drill that appears below, he manages only
to hit in sync the words that appear in bold.*)

VERY IMPORTANT CASSETTE TAPE & FRANK:
          "Here we go. Betty Botter bought some **butter** but she
          said this butter's **bitter** if I put it in my batter it
          will make my batter bitter so she bought a bit of
          better **butter** put it in her bitter batter made her
          bitter batter better so it's better Betty **Botter**
          bought a bit of better butter
          Ten ten twenty **twenty** thirty thirty forty forty fifty
          fifty sixty sixty seventy seventy **eighty eighty** ninety
          ninety ninety ninety eighty **eighty** seventy seventy
          sixty sixty fifty fifty forty forty **thirty** thirty twenty
          twenty ten ten

Betty Botter bought some **butter** but she said this butter's **bitter** if I put it in my batter it will make my batter bitter so she bought a bit of better **butter** put it in her bitter batter made her **bitter batter better** so it's better Betty **Botter** bought a bit of better butter

One one **one** and a quarter one and quarter one and a half one and a half seventy-five **seventy-five** Two two two and a quarter two and a quarter two and a half two and a half **seventy-five** seventy-five Three three three and a quarter three and a quarter three and a half three and a half seventy-five **seventy-five** Four four four and a quarter four and a quarter four and a half four and a half seventy-five **seventy-five** Five five five and a quarter five and a quarter five and a half five and a half seventy-five **seventy-five** Six six six and a quarter six and a quarter six and a half six and a half seventy-five **seventy-five** Seven seven seven and a quarter seven and a quarter seven and a half seven and a half seventy-five **seventy-five** Eight eight eight and a quarter eight and a quarter eight and a half eight and a half seventy-five **seventy-five** Nine nine nine and a quarter nine and a quarter nine and a half nine and a half seventy-five **seventy-five** Ten ten ten and a quarter ten and a quarter ten and a half ten and a half seventy-five **seventy-five**

Betty Botter bought some **butter** but she said this butter's **bitter** if I put it in my batter it will make my batter bitter so she bought a bit of better **butter** put it in her bitter batter made her **bitter batter better** so it's better Betty **Botter** bought a bit of better butter

Take a big hand for yourself and have a seat."

(BABETTE *is still on the phone.*)

BABETTE: It's it's
what it Is
is
a collection of Modern Era Outbursts It'll be a book of
of
Seminal Outbursts you know Outbursts that really
Went
Somewhere Got Something Done

BABETTE: And and I mean it's a very exciting project because
I mean if I do say so myself
a deconstruction of the Outburst could do a lot to
illuminate evolution itself
I mean
In My View
In My Book
The History Of The World
IS
The History Of The Outburst
Hang on Someone's at my door

(THEO *has abandoned his synthesizer, emerged from his apart-*
ment, and knocked on BABETTE's *door.* BABETTE *opens her door.*)

THEO: I need to talk

BABETTE: I'm on the phone

THEO: Good that's a start but I need you to talk to me

BABETTE: *(into phone)*
Can I call you back Theo's here m hm mm hmm
mmm hmmm zzactly bye Hi How's Thrill-o-rama

THEO: Boring I'm feeling very
Well am
I correct in understanding
that you're rejecting me

*(*BABETTE *has immediately shifted her focus to her rolls of coins,
and is offering* THEO *but a portion of her attention.)*

BABETTE: Just sexually

THEO: Oh phew

BABETTE: How foolish of me to assume that you value our
friendship

THEO: I value it so much that I want to enhance it

BABETTE: With sex

THEO: Intimacy in general

BABETTE: Intimacy is never general Theo

*(*THEO *mimics her, mouthing the words "Intimacy is
never general Theo."* BABETTE *doesn't notice.)*

THEO: Am I that repulsive

*(*BABETTE *actually considers this question for a
moment and then proceeds to think aloud.)*

BABETTE: It's Physics not Physical Theo by which I mean
you don't Disgust Me
you just exert a Repulsive Force for me on a
what
Molecular Level

THEO: Oh
So it's nothing personal

BABETTE: *(sincere)*
Not
At
All

(THEO *starts to leave.*)

BABETTE: Oh hey Theo
any spare quarters on ya I'm this close to a roll

(FRANK *practices.*)

FRANK   Belligerent Beulah bellowed bloody bombast
Belligerent Beulah bellowed bloody bombast
Belligerent Beulah bellowed bloody bombast

(THEO *plays around on the synthesizer.*
Eventually he begins to croon.)

THEO: Babette Babette you put
a hex on me
Babette Babette why not
have sex with me

(BABETTE, *pencil in hand, hovers over the manuscript*
of her "Outbursts Text" and reads aloud.)

BABETTE: 1457 A cell full of monks hunched over myriad ecclesiastical
texts they are diligently recopying
Brother Theodore Klotz stands suddenly as he hurtles his
quill to the stone floor and shouts
I'll Be Fucked If I'm Transcribing One More Word
The next day Brother Klotz visits his friend Johann Fust
son-in-law of Johann Gutenberg
They share a bottle of claret
Movable Metal Type is born

(Three bathrooms. BABETTE *is perched on the side of her bathtub. She is shaving her legs.* FRANK *and* THEO *are shaving their faces in their respective bathrooms. We see all three of them through the reflections of their mirrors.)*

FRANK: Why auctioneering I want my words to
            Succeed

BABETTE: When I went to work in an office I spent my day
            negotiating my way
            through a sea of people who kept
            repeating and repeating
            in one way or another
            the same five words
            The Mistake Is Not Mine

THEO: And I mean the whole experience of dissolution
            of dissolving leads one inevitably to try to
            identify The The
            Dissolvent because
            I thought we were profoundly happy Beth and I

FRANK: It's not that I plan to start using words like Humdinger
            or anything

THEO: I learned sadly enough that profound happiness is
                 itself a
            Dissolvent

BABETTE: The Mistake Is Not Mine

FRANK   It's not like I'll start walking around saying
            Mighty to modify Fine

THEO: I guess I just wish I was back at the skating rink

BABETTE: What I was never able to express
much to my regret is that the mistake
is precisely what is of Interest

(BABETTE, FRANK, *and* THEO *all cut themselves shaving.*)

(THEO *is procrastinating.* FRANK *knocks on his door.* THEO
opens his door and FRANK *enters* THEO*'s apartment.*)

THEO: I'm composing what's up

(FRANK *sits down and plays a tune on* THEO*'s synthesizer.*)

FRANK: What if it went something like that

THEO: Have you been thinking about this

FRANK: It just came to me

THEO: I don't think it's right It's not
bad it's good but it's not
Thrill-o-rama

FRANK: Okay

THEO: I appreciate the thought

FRANK: Okay

THEO: I'll know Thrill-o-rama when I
hear it in my head

FRANK: Okay

THEO: It's not that I haven't been thinking
about it It's all that I think about when
I'm not thinking about having sex with Babette

FRANK: Okay

THEO: I appreciate the gesture but you see
         Thrill-o-rama the Gestalt of
         Thrill-o-rama is not reducible to
         some formula some expected formula
         I'm operating under the assumption that
         Thrill-o-rama the ride is thrilling
         because it's thrilling in an unexpected
         way and does not simply rehash a
         familiarly thrilling type ride experience
         The music needs to reflect this Frank

FRANK: Okay

THEO: Thrill-o-rama the melody can't be
         obviously thrilling In fact I'm coming
         to believe that it should be in fact
         seemingly boring so as to enhance the
         rush of the thrill experience when
         it is finally manifest I'm not
         criticizing but your Little Tune does
         not adequately subvert the thrill
         expectation

FRANK: Okay

THEO: And that is after all what we're
         doing here I mean I'm doing here I'm
         subverting the thrill expectation in order to
         intensify the rush of the ride Thrill-o-rama's
         not a simple thrill Frank

FRANK: Okay

THEO: It's a complex thrill It's a layered
         thrill It's as enigmatic as well as
         can be

FRANK: Okay

THEO: Okay so I appreciate as I said the
         effort on your part I'm flattered
         that Thrill-o-rama and my
         opus even appear as a Blip On Your
         Screen but Frank I'm sorry Frank
         Thrill-o-rama is something you Just
         Don't Grasp

FRANK: Okay

THEO: Okay

FRANK: Okay may I

         (FRANK *crosses to the synthesizer and plays another
         catchy tune—even catchier, of course, than the last.*)

FRANK: I mean that was the other one I was
         wondering about I don't know I mean
         obviously you're the composer and I
         hardly play

THEO: Frank Frank Frank uh how did you I
         mean when did you come up with these
         little little ditties

FRANK: I don't know I guess I was in the
         checkout line flipping through a
         magazine wondering what I was
         forgetting to buy having forgotten my list at home
         trying to recall the subject of my thesis paper in college
         while trying also to pinpoint the precise
         moment when my relationship with my father
         went Sour when they just uh
         Popped Into My Head

THEO: Exactly Frank exactly They just Popped
          Into Your Head Is that how you think
          this works Is that what you think
          composing's all about

FRANK: No I

THEO: Do you think I don't think of phrases
          all day as I'm working That's what
          they're called by the way Frank phrases musical
          phrases Do you think musical phrases
          and I mean Super Involved Really Complex
          musical phrases aren't Popping as you
          say into my head all the time

FRANK: No I

THEO: Because they are Frank They are but
          I don't even let myself actually play these
          Trifles on the keyboard because
          I don't want to Violate the keyboard's
          Integrity If it's not right it's not
          right Why waste time Do you think I'm
          interested in wasting time

FRANK: No I

THEO: That's right I'm not and I'll tell you
          why Frank Because these people
          these Amusement Park People are
          Professionals okay These Amusement Park People
          mean Serious Business okay and that means they're
          not interested in messing around with
          Amateurs and that's why they hired me
          a Professional to lovingly sculpt an
          appropriately Weighty not to mention
          Mysterious score for Thrill-o-rama Sure

they could have hired Some Hack but they
wanted the job Done Right They wanted
a classically trained composer who attended a genuine
    School
of Music
or or Conservatory as we say in the field to
craft a melody as memorable as Thrill-
o-rama is sure to be for the average pimply prepubes-
    cent who
rides it
Are you saying the average pimply prepubescent
doesn't deserve a real musical score
for his Amusement Park Ride Experience

FRANK: No I

THEO: Of course the average pimply prepubescent
          deserves a real musical score and I
          know you don't mean disrespect

FRANK: No I

THEO: There's no shame in what you've done

FRANK: No I

THEO: I forgive you Frank

FRANK: Okay

THEO: I forgive you but if you ever ever approach
          my keyboard again without an express
          invitation from me to do so I will be
          forced to Kick Your Ass No No I won't
          kick your ass I'll Break Your Fingers
          That would be more appropriate don't
          you think

FRANK: Okay

THEO: I don't mean to be insulting

FRANK: Okay

THEO: No hard feelings

FRANK: No

THEO: Okay

FRANK: Okay so you don't want to hear the third tune I
            thought up right

            (BABETTE is on the phone.)

BABETTE: *(into phone, fluid)*
            Well I like her
            Or I want to like her
            Because other people I like like her
            But the truth is

BABETTE: *(into phone)*
            I don't like her

            (There is a knock at BABETTE's door.)

BABETTE: *(into phone)*
            Just a second there's someone at my door

       (BABETTE answers the door; FRANK is standing outside of it.)

BABETTE: I'm on the phone Frank

FRANK: Can I sit in your apartment Babette

BABETTE: Why

FRANK: My cats need some space

> (BABETTE *opens the door wide so that* FRANK *can enter and then immediately returns to her phone conversation.*)

BABETTE: *(into phone)*
But then I think Why don't I like her
Do I not like her because I think she doesn't like me
which I do think
or do I not like her because I can't relate to her
intellectually
But if I can't relate to her intellectually is that because
she's smarter or Stupider OR are we in fact such
intellectual equals
that we can't recognize the intelligence of the other so
blinded are we by the reflection of comparable
thought
But frankly

FRANK: *(did you say my name)*
Yes

BABETTE: *(continuing into phone)*
I don't think that's it
and anyway the larger question is
Why Do I Want To Like Her

FRANK: *(said simultaneously with Babette's line)*
Why Do You Want To Like Her

BABETTE: *(into phone)*
and I have to say that I don't think I actually have Any
Interest in liking her
I Just Want Her To Like Me

FRANK: *(said simultaneously with Babette's line)*
You Just Want Her To Like You

BABETTE: *(into phone)*
          and and
          of course the truly haunting aspect of all of this is that
          All Of The People I Like Like Her

FRANK: *(said simultaneously with Babette's line)*
          All Of The People You Like Like Her

BABETTE: *(into phone)*
          At The Same Time As They Like Me
          so so
          Where does the true affection lie and
          well okay I guess I do recall ONE MOMENT when
          I Thought I Liked Her when we happened to be in a
          bathroom at
          the same time and of course there was no toilet paper
              in the stall to which I had gravitated and she
              somehow psychically sensed my predicament and
              passed some toilet paper to me under the stall and
              in that moment
          okay
          I actually Loved Her but

FRANK: WHAT ABOUT MY DESIRES

                    (SLIGHT PAUSE.)

BABETTE: *(into phone)*
          Frank I'm on the phone Oh you do Okay Okay Talk to
          you soon

              (BABETTE *hangs up the phone.*)

BABETTE: Shoot
          I forgot to ask her something

FRANK: The thing is Babette that it's not a matter
           of talking fast it's a matter of
           fast talkin' It's a different thing entirely

           (SLIGHT PAUSE.)

FRANK: Is it okay if I vacuum

BABETTE: Feel free Frank Nice shirt

FRANK: Thanks

           (FRANK crosses to a closet and pulls out an old
                   pink vacuum cleaner.)

BABETTE: Where'd you get it

FRANK: I don't
           know I picked it up somewhere

(FRANK plugs in the vacuum and begins vacuuming. He makes a
long horizontal cross. He is a graceful vacuumer. He makes another
long horizontal cross and then pauses to pick up a piece of paper
from the carpet. He turns the vacuum off as he reads.)

FRANK: When um did you receive This

BABETTE: What

FRANK: This um this invitation to Larry's
           Party

BABETTE: I don't know Recently

FRANK: I wasn't invited

BABETTE: Really

FRANK: You know I wasn't invited

BABETTE: I've seen that shirt before

FRANK: Larry thinks I'm not handling this break-up well
             He thinks I can't handle seeing him
             Is Theo invited

BABETTE: I don't know

(FRANK *moves toward the door.*)

BABETTE: Yes

FRANK: Did you know I wasn't invited

BABETTE: Where have I seen that shirt before

FRANK: Are you going to go

BABETTE: Possibly

FRANK: Is Theo going

BABETTE: How should I know

FRANK: All he thinks about is having sex with you

BABETTE: I thought you were here to vacuum

(FRANK *begins vacuuming again.* BABETTE *continues
to watch* FRANK. FRANK *stops vacuuming in order to
move something out of the way.*)

FRANK: Boy when was the last time you vacuumed

BABETTE: Boy I don't remember

(The phone rings.)

BABETTE: *(into phone)*
Hello Hi I didn't forget What would
you like me to bring Okay Great but
I'm Kind Of In The Middle Of Something
Okay I'll talk to you later when I'm less
Right

(BABETTE *hangs up the phone.*)

FRANK: Was that Larry Babette

(SLIGHT PAUSE.)

FRANK   Please just answer my question Babette

BABETTE: And then will you

FRANK: *(cutting her off)*
Yes Babette

BABETTE: *(cutting him off)*
Yes Frank

(FRANK *begins to vacuum again as* BABETTE *continues to watch him. After a few moments of vigorous
vacuuming in a corner,* FRANK *turns off the vacuum.*)

FRANK: Did Larry tell you not to tell me about
The Party

BABETTE: You just

FRANK: *(cutting her off)*
Did he

BABETTE: No

FRANK: Did he

BABETTE: Yes

(FRANK *begins vacuuming again. There is a knock at* BABETTE'*s door. Neither* BABETTE *nor* FRANK *hears the knock, so there is a bang on* BABETTE'*s door.* FRANK *turns off the vacuum.*)

FRANK: I'll get it Babette

BABETTE: Super Frank

                    (FRANK *opens the door. It's* THEO.)

THEO: Oh I was looking for Babette

FRANK: She's right over there

THEO: What are you doing here

FRANK: Vacuuming

THEO: Oh Have you been talking about me

FRANK/BABETTE:
          Yes/No

THEO: I wanted to ask Babette something
          but I'll come back later

FRANK: Yes

THEO: What

FRANK: She's going to Larry's Party to which everyone in the
          world was invited except me

THEO: Great I'll see you there Babette

(The scene is over, but then suddenly it isn't as BABETTE *realizes:)*

BABETTE: I know where I've seen that shirt
On Mrs. Jorgenson

(The scene is over. FRANK *practices.)*

FRANK: At least leave the lederhosen
At least leave the lederhosen
At least leave the lederhosen

THE INTERROGATION SCENE

*(*BABETTE, THEO, *and* FRANK *are in*
FRANK*'s apartment.)*

FRANK: Who else was there

THEO: Peter

FRANK: Peter Larry hates Peter

BABETTE: Not that Peter another Peter you don't know

FRANK: A Peter I don't know Does
Larry like Peter-I-don't-know

THEO   He likes him but he doesn't like-like him

BABETTE: It wouldn't matter This Peter this other Peter doesn't
like-like boys

FRANK: Oh so Larry found him captivating no doubt Was
Clarissa there

BABETTE: No

THEO: Yes she was She just didn't stay long because Joseph
                 was there with his new girlfriend

BABETTE: I didn't talk to her Did you talk to her

THEO: Clarissa or the new girlfriend

FRANK: WAS IT FUN

THEO: No

BABETTE: No

FRANK: Are you lying

BABETTE: Yes

THEO: Yes

FRANK: Was it Very fun

BABETTE: Yes

THEO: Yes

FRANK: Was it the best party you've ever been to

THEO: The best

BABETTE: Yes

FRANK: Are you lying

BABETTE/THEO:
                 (face the truth, damn it/unable to lie)
                 No

BABETTE: I don't like this game

THEO: Me neither

FRANK: In my sandbox I make the rules Did my name
        cross Larry's lips

THEO: We weren't standing beside him all night Frank

BABETTE: We also weren't standing beside each other

THEO: Much to my chagrin

FRANK: Meanwhile back to Larry's lips

BABETTE: Well I did hear him say Frank as I was on my way to
        the bathroom once but he might've just been saying
        frank-ly

THEO: He does say that word a lot

BABETTE: For emphasis It's true

FRANK: How many people were there total

BABETTE: Ooh I don't know Two fifty

FRANK: Two hunderd n fitty

THEO: Two fifty
        Three

FRANK: Half the city in other words

BABETTE: Not half

THEO: It was pretty intimate actually I
            mean the conversations were intimate

BABETTE: That's true but there was a sort of
            expansiveness to people's talk that
            gave you that Anything's Possible feeling

THEO: I know what you mean The chit-chat had a
            weight to it that somehow managed to avoid pretension

BABETTE: I didn't encounter one especially obnoxious person

THEO: And I was impressed with the array of people's
            accomplishments I mean that was one diverse group of
            people

BABETTE: But still there wasn't a single conversation that made
            me
            feel hopeless in terms of my own achievements or
            goals and
            actually I witnessed several people receive quality job
            offers from partygoers they'd just met

THEO: Oh yes people were supportive

BABETTE: And fun

THEO: It was the most supportive and fun party No question

BABETTE: No question

THEO: In every case as far as I'm aware the conversation
            transcended what people had in common

BABETTE: Definitely
            And there was none of the usual Floating Party Anxiety

THEO: God no

BABETTE: It was a peaceful party

THEO: And never a line for the bathroom

BABETTE: And never a shortage of food

THEO: or drink

BABETTE: And not too smoky

THEO: And not too hot

BABETTE: And not too crowded

THEO: And no trouble locating one's belongings when it was
          time to go

BABETTE: My coat was on the top of the pile

THEO: Mine too And someone had stuck twenty bucks in my
          pocket

          (SLIGHT PAUSE. *The hint of a sigh.*)

BABETTE & THEO:
          (there will never be another like it)
          It was the most supportive and fun party ever No
          question

(BABETTE, THEO, *and* FRANK *are situated at their respective
windows listening to the* AIRSHAFT COUPLE, *from whose apartment we hear the sound of shower water running. The man calls to
the woman from outside of the bathroom.*)

MAN'S VOICE:
          Why am I leaving again

WOMAN'S VOICE:
> What

MAN'S VOICE:
> Why am I leaving again

>> *(The water is turned off.)*

WOMAN'S VOICE:
> Pass me

>> *(She cuts herself off as the man has thrown the woman her towel.)*

> Thanks

MAN'S VOICE:
> Why am I leaving again

WOMAN'S VOICE:
> You're not leaving again you're
> leaving for the first time

MAN'S VOICE:
> Tell me again why I'm leaving

WOMAN'S VOICE:
> Because
> your strange isn't my strange

MAN'S VOICE:
> I would hope not

WOMAN'S VOICE:
> Oh

MAN'S VOICE:
>   *(what I mean is)*
>   I would hope not

WOMAN'S VOICE:
>   Oh

(BABETTE, pencil in hand, is poring over her "Outbursts Text.")

BABETTE: 6 28 1914 the wife of Archduke Francis Ferdinand sug-
>   gests a Sunday drive in Sarajevo
>   Suddenly the duchess begins to feel faint and
>   Ferdinand instructs their driver to run into a
>   Slavic shop to purchase an ice cold beverage
>   Several seconds after a young Bosnian nationalist
>   emerges from the store sipping a drink the driver
>   returns to the vehicle to explain that the young
>   Bosnian nationalist got the last ice cold beverage
>   in town
>   The outraged Archduke cries out after the young
>   Bosnian nationalist
>   The Duchess Had Dibs On That Ice Cold Balkan
>   Beverage
>   The young Bosnian nationalist pauses to take a long
>   sip before he fires fatal shots into both Ferdinand
>   and his thirsty wife
>   World War I begins

(There is a knock at BABETTE's door. She opens it.)

THEO: Could you come over for a few minutes It
>   won't take long I promise not to beg you to
>   be my girlfriend

*(THEO leaves. BABETTE exits her apartment immediately
thereafter and knocks on THEO's door. He opens it.)*

THEO: What brings you here Kidding Why don't you have a seat

BABETTE: To keep Really

THEO: Ha ha So uh as you know it's been a while since since

BABETTE: Recall

THEO: Since the uh mysterious disappearance of my
                 Beth

BABETTE: Uh huh

THEO: And uh and uh well I'm beginning to
                 think her departure is going to stick
                 That is I'm beginning to believe that
                 she's not coming back

BABETTE: Yeah she's not

THEO: Beth's not coming back and so I've
                 decided that I'd like you to have
                 her things

BABETTE: What do you mean by that exactly

THEO: She left most of her things here I want you to have
                 them

BABETTE: Why

THEO: It seems silly for them to go unused

BABETTE: Give them away

THEO: That's what I'm attempting to do

BABETTE: Why me

THEO: You're my
            friend

BABETTE: Have you ever seen *Rebecca*

THEO: Yes

BABETTE: Is this a *Rebecca* thing

THEO: Beth had some nice things clothes
            and I thought since money's tight you
            might want to take a look at them and
            see if there's anything that you would
            enjoy having that's all

BABETTE: Is that the pile over there Did you
            make that pile

THEO: I gathered a few of her
            things together

BABETTE: I don't know that I want her things

THEO: She was nice You would have liked her

BABETTE: She abandoned you

THEO: Something must've been afoot I
            should've known when she lost her wedding
            ring

BABETTE: When did you start saying afoot

THEO: Just now I think

BABETTE: What do you mean she lost her wedding
            ring

THEO: I thought she'd use the insurance
            money to have another one made but
            she spent it otherwise it turns out

BABETTE: On what

THEO: Luggage I later discovered Pick out some stuff

   (BABETTE *starts to go through the pile of Beth's belongings.*)

BABETTE: This is a nice coat

THEO: Try it on

                    (BABETTE *tries on the coat.*)

THEO: It looks good on you

BABETTE: It doesn't make me look short bulky or pale

            (THEO *shakes his head twice in response to the first
      two but admits, through subtle facial expression, that
              the coat MIGHT make her look pale.*)

BABETTE: You aren't getting rid of that couch are you

THEO: No

BABETTE: You shouldn't it looks really good in there
            This is a pretty dress

THEO: She was wearing that when I proposed
            the first time Try this on over it That's
            the way she always wore it

BABETTE: There's a piece of paper in the pocket

THEO: What is it

BABETTE: It's a To Do list

THEO: What does it say

BABETTE: Pick up dry cleaning
         Return library books
         Leave The

THEO: Leave The

BABETTE: Leave the O
         Oh Leave Theo
         I couldn't read the O at first

THEO: Um will you be my girlfriend

(FRANK practices.)

FRANK: Mother made me mysterious meat at mealtime mostly
           Mother made me mysterious meat at mealtime mostly
           Mother made me mysterious meat at mealtime mostly

(In the hallway. FRANK *and* THEO *stand near* FRANK*'s door.)*

THEO: Two weeks in Kansas City

FRANK: Plus the countless hours with the at-home training
           tape and manual

THEO: Oh that's what that noise was

FRANK: Noise

THEO: Sound

(BABETTE appears from the stairwell.)

BABETTE: Hi guys I just picked up the photos from my trip The
          real photos this time My little friend at the Quick
          Clicks found them Wanna see

THEO & FRANK:
          Sure but maybe later I have to go take care of
          something

(FRANK *stands in between the doorways of* THEO *and* BABETTE*'s
apartments. When he speaks,* FRANK *adopts a bad southern
accent, or maybe several. Throughout the auction* BABETTE *will
continue to attempt to work on her "Outbursts Text" and* THEO
will continue to attempt to compose on his synthesizer.)

FRANK: All right we're gonna open the bidding at one fifty

BABETTE: What's for sale Frank

FRANK: Colonel
          A fact

THEO & BABETTE:
          Like what

FRANK: A Fact each of you would like to know and Don't

THEO: The same Fact Frank

FRANK: Colonel A different Fact One each

BABETTE & THEO:
          You've been keeping Facts from us Frank

FRANK   New Facts
          Colonel
          Brand spanking new Facts

BABETTE: How do you determine a winner

FRANK: The bidding will stop when this piece of gum I will
         now place on the ceiling loses its stickiness and falls to
         the floor All right we're gonna open the bidding at one
         fitty

BABETTE: One fifty

FRANK: One fitty one fitty over here it's one fitty

THEO: One seventy-five

FRANK: Senty-five senty-five
         do I hear
         two hunderd two hunderd

BABETTE: Two hundred

FRANK: Two hunderd two hunderd

THEO: Two twenty-five

FRANK: Tweny-five tweny-five ana quarter ana quarter

BABETTE: Fifty

FRANK: Two naf two naf

THEO: Seventy-five

FRANK: Three-quarter three-quarter
         senty-five senty-five

THEO: (said simultaneously with Babette)
         Three

BABETTE: *(said simultaneously with Theo)*
          Three three

FRANK: And the lady three hunderd three hunderd

THEO: FOUR HUNDRED

FRANK: Four hunderd four hunderd
          Do I hear
          OH
          The gum has fallen and the bidding has closed at
          Four Hunderd Dollars
          Sold to the Man At The Synthesizer

BABETTE: What about my Fact

THEO: *(this is old news)*
          The gum has fallen Babette

FRANK: There'll be other auctions Little Lady

THEO: Forget about her Fact Colonel What's my Fact

FRANK: All right well your Fact
          your Brand Spanking New Fact is this
          I saw Beth on the street yesterday

THEO: My
          Beth reappeared
          Did you speak to her

FRANK: Yes I spoke to her but that's not all
          There's more

THEO: A lot more

FRANK: She was with Larry

THEO & BABETTE:
>   Larry

FRANK: They've been in touch and strange as this will sound
I suspect they've been touching

THEO & BABETTE:
>   Larry and Beth have been touching
Ew

THEO: What did my
Beth say

FRANK: She lives here She never left town

THEO & BABETTE:
>   Wow

FRANK: She had a message for you

THEO: What

FRANK: She wants to come by and
pick up her things

*(BABETTE, FRANK, and THEO lie in their respective
beds. FRANK and THEO are asleep. With hand gestures,
BABETTE makes elaborate shadows on the ceiling.)*

BABETTE:
>   As children my brothers and I had a toboggan we
called Jeremiah
Last night as I was sledding down a sand dune in my
dream Jeremiah told me to Get The Hell Off

*(BABETTE turns to go to sleep as FRANK wakes
up and begins to make shadows.)*

FRANK: I was born on the third story of a
            hospital and grew up on the third story of a
            house and today live on the third story of an
            apartment building
            I've always inhabited the third story

            *(FRANK turns to go to sleep as THEO wakes up
            and begins to make shadows.)*

THEO: When I met her I told Beth I want to be the one you'd
            sleep with if you didn't have a girlfriend already I
            want to be first in line I couldn't find the line I thought
            Ah I must create the line I didn't know where to stand
            I picked a spot and waited for a long long time We
            kept in touch at a safe distance and then Beth finally
            gave up and let me step out of
            line

            *(THEO turns to go to sleep as BABETTE wakes up and
            begins to make shadows.)*

BABETTE: In other words I had a dream Theo didn't want to be
          my friend anymore

            (FRANK wakes up and joins BABETTE in making shadows.)

FRANK: Don't use other words

            *(THEO wakes up and joins BABETTE and
            FRANK in making shadows.)*

THEO: Pick the right ones

            *(FRANK suddenly sits up in his bed and makes a very
            speedy, greatly enunciated speech.)*

FRANK: Cut the cake cut the crap the cardinal can't come over
          Cut the cake cut the crap the cardinal can't come over
          Cut the cake cut the crap the cardinal can't come over
          Peachy keen Peach pit
          Peachy keen Peach pit
          Peachy keen Peach Pit
          Theda thought the thigh was thawed but it was
              thoroughly tholid
          Theda thought the thigh was thawed but it was
              thoroughly tholid
          Theda thought the thigh was thawed but it was
              thoroughly tholid
          Romance is really rather a riddle
          Romance is really rather a riddle
          Romance is really rather a riddle

                   (BABETTE *knocks on* FRANK's *door. He answers it.*)

BABETTE: I've come for my Fact

FRANK: You can't have your Fact
          Not just like that

BABETTE: I'm not bidding for it

FRANK: Suit yourself

BABETTE: Who else would I suit

                        (FRANK's *door closes.*)

BABETTE: Fine I have a Fact too
          About You

                        (FRANK's *door opens.*)

FRANK: What Fact

BABETTE: It's not a Fact exactly
It's an opinion
but it's Deeply Held

FRANK: By whom

BABETTE: By Larry

FRANK: What's Larry's opinion

BABETTE: What's your Fact

FRANK: You first

BABETTE: Same time

FRANK: Fine

BABETTE: On the count of three

FRANK: One

BABETTE: After three or On three

FRANK: After One

BABETTE: Two

FRANK: Three

BABETTE: *(said simultaneously with Frank)*
Larry says you've gone off the deep end

FRANK: *(said simultaneously with Babette)*
Larry feels sorry for you

BABETTE & FRANK:
Pardon

BABETTE: *(said simultaneously with Frank)*
          Larry says your dreams of auctioneering are ridiculous

FRANK: *(said simultaneously with Babette)*
          Larry says you can't keep your word

BABETTE & FRANK:
          What

BABETTE: *(said simultaneously with Frank)*
          Larry thinks you're a fool

FRANK: *(said simultaneously with Babette)*
          Larry thinks you're a fool

                    (SLIGHT PAUSE.)

BABETTE & FRANK:
          Oh

(BABETTE, FRANK, and THEO sit in their apartment next to the phone. At once the three of them pick up the phone, dial a number—we should hear the sound of the individual number tones—and hang up in frustration, the number they have dialed apparently busy. After a moment, simultaneously inspired, the three of them dial another number, only to find that number busy as well. All three hang up the phone in frustration.)

(In the hallway. Ideally, the following is scored by Fats Domino's version of "Kansas City." THEO and BABETTE stand in their doorways. FRANK, dressed in an old-fashioned suit and bow tie, walks down the hall, suitcase in hand, offering a small wave.)

BABETTE: You don't just leave without saying goodbye Frank

FRANK: Goodbye Frank

BABETTE: Goodbye Frank

THEO: Goodbye Colonel

*(Theo enters his apartment and Babette remains where she is
as Frank descends the stairs and then ascends them a VERY
short while later, during which time the music should have
faded somewhat and then increased in volume again, according
to Frank's whereabouts. The music stops abruptly.)*

BABETTE: Hi Frank
         How was it

FRANK: I don't wish to discuss it

BABETTE: Why

FRANK: *(isn't it obvious)*
         My talkin' doesn't have any legs all right

BABETTE: Oh

                 (THEO emerges from his apartment.)

THEO: Hi Frank

BABETTE: He's not discussing it

THEO: Why Frank

BABETTE: *(isn't it obvious)*
         His talkin' doesn't have any legs all right

THEO: Wow

(FRANK is hanging outside of BABETTE's window. He wears a window-washing harness and is cleaning her window. BABETTE opens her window and leans outside. THEO stands next to her.)

BABETTE: **Would you care for something to drink Frank**

THEO: **Babette I need**—to talk to you about a rather delicate matter

(THEO closes the window so that we miss the rest of his line. BABETTE starts to speak before she reopens the window so that we miss the first part of her line. Throughout the scene, all we hear is the text that appears in bold.)

BABETTE: Listen Theo whatever you have—**to say you can say in front of Frank**

THEO: **Frank doesn't**—want to hear the content of this rather delicate matter

(Once again, THEO closes the window so that we miss the second half of his line, and once again BABETTE starts to speak before she reopens the window, so that we miss the first part of her line.)

BABETTE: Frank does—**too want to hear it**

(THEO immediately closes the window; we miss the first part of his line but then hear the rest after BABETTE reopens the window. The pattern continues.)

THEO: Listen Babette the fact of the matter is—**I need those things I gave you back You know the coat the dress and the thing that goes over the dress that makes it an outfit**

(THEO closes the window; BABETTE claps during the first part of her line. By the end of her line BABETTE reopens the window.)

BABETTE: Oh that is great just great I'm so proud of you but you
know what the answer is Theo the answer is—**Forget it**

FRANK: **Could you**

(THEO *closes the window by the end of his line.*)

THEO: **Please she asked about those items speci**—fically

(BABETTE *opens the window by the end of her line.*)

BABETTE: How many times can one person be taken Answer me
that You—**owe her nothing**

(THEO *closes the window, and* BABETTE *reopens
it shortly thereafter.*)

THEO: **Look Listen**—there's something you need to under-
stand Beth's a truly dan—**gerous woman She's got a
really bad temper**

(THEO *closes,* BABETTE *opens,* THEO *almost closes,*
BABETTE *reopens the window.*)

BABETTE: **You are so pre**—dictable just so utterly fu—**cking**—
pre—**dictable**

FRANK: **Um could you**

THEO: **Frank do you think I should call someone**

BABETTE: **Frank do you think he should call his mommy**

(*Again, a struggle at the window ensues.*)

THEO: **I am asking you for the**—last time as a—
gentleman—would ask a lady if you would please—
gimme back—my ex-wife's personal be—**longings**

BABETTE: **N-o The-o**

FRANK: **It would actually help if the window remained closed**

BABETTE: **You want the coat**

(THEO *nods and closes the window.* BABETTE *finds the coat and opens the window halfway into her line.*)

BABETTE: Here's—**the coat**

(BABETTE *throws the coat out the window.* FRANK *catches it.* THEO *closes the window,* BABETTE *opens it,* THEO *closes it and* BABETTE *opens it again.*)

BABETTE: **Oh and here's**—you know lady to gentleman **Beth's dress**

(BABETTE *unzips the dress she is wearing. She steps out of it and throws it out the window.*)

BABETTE: **Would you mind not staring at my breasts Theo when I'm trying to make an interpersonal point**

(FRANK *is deeply philosophical.*)

FRANK: They'd have us believe that a certain Betty Botter Just Happened to buy a bit of bitter butter that she was foolish enough to add to her batter and that then this Betty this same Betty Botter attempted to rectify the situation by buying better butter to add to her already ruined batter
Frankly
I'm coming to suspect Betty's motives were purely alliterative

(THEO *dramatically lifts a hand and almost plays a note. He holds
his finger above the key for an extended period of time before, after
deep thought, he reconsiders and quite definitely almost plays
another note. He then, slowly at first and eventually in a mad fren-
zy, reaches the cusp of playing a dozen notes only to change his
mind each time at the last possible moment. Finally,* THEO *plays
the same few bars of his composition but then miraculously continues to play, only to realize, as should we, that he is playing a famil-
iar tune not of his composition, perhaps Kurt Weill's "Mack the
Knife." An extended and strange outburst, a sound of unique
anguish and frustration, emerges from* THEO. *Silence.*)

(THEO *knocks on* BABETTE's *door. She opens it.*)

THEO: Hi
        FYI
        I don't want you to be my girlfriend anymore

(Night. FRANK, BABETTE, *and* THEO *are lying on their backs on
the roof of their building. They are staring at the sky.)*

THEO: Do you wanna play Choose Your Parents

BABETTE & FRANK:
        Nah

BABETTE: Anyway Theo it's called Choose Your Ancestry It's
         about Deep Lineage
         not just one generation

         (SLIGHT PAUSE.)

FRANK: Actually Babette I made up the game
         It is called Choose Your Parents

         (SLIGHT PAUSE.)

BABETTE: Do you wanna play All The Conversations I Don't
          Want To Have

THEO & FRANK:
          Nah

THEO: All The Conversations I Don't Want To Have takes for-
          ever and
          Besides
          I'd rather not discuss that game

FRANK: Do you wanna play Do You Smell Something Burning

BABETTE & THEO:
          Nah

FRANK: What about I Either Left The Iron Plugged In Or The
          Door Unlocked I Just Know It

BABETTE: I Either Left The Iron Plugged In Or The Door
          Unlocked I Just Know It gets too personal

THEO & FRANK:
          It does

THEO: What about My Favorite People Should Be Your
          Favorite People

FRANK: No
          Way
          My Favorite People Should Be Your Favorite People is
          inherently homophobic and I'm not sorry if I'm
          offending whoever thought of it

THEO & BABETTE:
          You thought of it Frank

          (SLIGHT PAUSE.)

THEO: How about a round of Landlord Go Home or a little
           Landlord Gimme Back My Rent

FRANK: Or Excuse Me You Annoy Me

BABETTE: Or Mi Casa Is Not Su Casa

THEO: Or Teacher's Doubts Panned Out

BABETTE: I told you I wasn't playing Teacher's Doubts Panned
           Out anymore

THEO: Shitty prescient bastards

FRANK: What about Where Were You Really

THEO: What about I Saw You Go Into A Restaurant After You
           Said You Weren't Hungry

BABETTE: You always want to play that game

FRANK: What about The People With Whom I've Blown It

THEO & BABETTE:
           Oh please Frank We don't have all night

BABETTE: What about The People I Meant To Sleep With

THEO & FRANK:
           Oh please Babette We don't have all night

FRANK: What about The People Who Never Got Back To Me

THEO: What about Could You Cloak Your Animosity A Little
           I Just Woke Up

FRANK: What about I'm Lousy With Unrequited Love i.e. I
Have Utterly No One To Kiss

THEO & BABETTE:
How do you play that

FRANK: Oh I thought for sure you could tell me

THEO: How about Stop Saying Cinema When You Know You
Mean Movie and Other Pretentious Words

FRANK: What about Larry's game

THEO & BABETTE:
You mean Grand Rationalization

FRANK: I mean Larry's Other Game

THEO & BABETTE:
You Mean Best Friend

(SLIGHT PAUSE.)

BABETTE: *(how could you)*
I'm sorry but I can't believe you suggested that Frank

THEO: *(yeah how could you)*
I really can't either

(SLIGHT PAUSE.)

FRANK: I'm sorry I
momentarily forgot what happened last time

THEO: Some of my hair still hasn't grown back

FRANK: Mine neither

BABETTE: Whose has

(PAUSE.)

*(They are quiet and stare some more at the sky; the silence
is interrupted by the* AIRSHAFT COUPLE, *who are standing in awkward relation to each other—visible only in
shadow—in the front doorway of their apartment.)*

WOMAN'S VOICE:
    So do you

MAN'S VOICE:
    Why does it matter

WOMAN'S VOICE:
    I need to know Do you

MAN'S VOICE:
    Maybe

WOMAN'S VOICE:
    Maybe

MAN'S VOICE:
    Yes

WOMAN'S VOICE:
    You Maybe forgive me

(PAUSE.)

MAN'S VOICE:
    Hon it's the best I can do

(PAUSE.)

(THEO, BABETTE, and FRANK suddenly sit up as they share a simultaneous recollection.)

BABETTE & FRANK & THEO:
MRS. JORGENSON

(A SNEEZE FROM THE AIRSHAFT. FRANK, THEO, and BABETTE wait. Then:)

FRANK & THEO & BABETTE:
Bless you

(BLACKOUT.)

END

MELISSA JAMES GIBSON has been awarded a National Endowment for the Arts/Theatre Communications Group Playwriting Residency; grants from the New York State Council on the Arts and the Greenwall Foundation; fellowships from the Jerome Foundation and the MacDowell Colony; and commissions from the Steppenwolf Theatre Company and The Children's Theatre Company—where her play *Brooklyn Bridge* will receive its world premiere during the 2003-04 season. She has also written and co-directed a twenty-minute black-and-white film, *Given Fish*, which is contained within a play of the same name. Her work, including [sic] and *Suitcase, or those that resemble flies from a distance*, has been developed and/or produced at Soho Rep, as well as at PlayLabs, A.S.K. Theatre Projects, and Roadworks Productions, among other venues. A graduate of the Yale School of Drama, she earned her B.A. at Columbia University. Melissa James Gibson teaches playwriting at Saint Ann's School, in Brooklyn, and is a member of New Dramatists.